A bit of oil

Nat and Sam are at Nan
and Pop's. Pop is digging
the soil.

Nat cannot shut the lock. It is too tight. So Pop gets his old oil tin.

A bit of oil will fix it.

Then Pop looks at the chain.
Pop tips oil on the chain.

Now the chain
will turn well.

Sam tells Pop that the
bell has worn out.

Pop fixes that too.

Then Pop adds oil to his car.

That will fix it.

Pop tips a bit of oil on this
and a bit of oil on that.

He tells us, "Lots of things
need a bit of oil to go well."

Pop finishes up and
sits his oil tin down.
We all go in.

Nan is cooking. She has
eggs on the boil and
chicken cooling on foil.

Nan cannot get the lid off a jar. Pop picks up the oil.

Then Nan mixes up a
salad. We all sit down.

Pop fills his dish with
chicken and salad.

He looks at us all and
tells us that his salad
will need a bit of...

...lemon!

Words to blend

shut	finishes	dish
tight	too	cooling
chain	turn	worn
that	this	things
need	car	jar
down	cooking	chicken
lock	ting	salad

Before reading

Synopsis: Pop is good at fixing things. He uses his oil to fix all kinds of things that aren't working properly.

Review graphemes/phonemes: ar or ur ow

New grapheme/phoneme: oi

Story discussion: Look at the cover and read the title together. Ask: *What has Pop got in his hand?* (an oil can) *What do you think he's doing with it?* (oiling a pair of shears) Check that children understand that oil can sometimes be used to loosen things that are stuck, or make things work more smoothly.

Link to prior learning: Display the grapheme *oi*. Say: *These two letters are a digraph – that means they make one sound.* Write or display these words: *foil, soil, boil, coil, coin*. How quickly can children identify the *oi* grapheme and read the words?

Vocabulary check: chain – on a bike the chain helps the wheels to turn

Decoding practice: Turn to page 11. How quickly can children find and read two words with *oi (foil, boil)*?

Tricky word practice: Display the word *go* and ask children to circle the tricky part of the word (*o*, which makes a long /oa/ sound). Practise writing and reading this word.

After reading

Apply learning: Ask: *What was the surprise at the end of the story?* (We expected Pop to put oil on his salad, but he used lemon instead!)

Comprehension

- Did Pop use the same oil for everything?

- What did Pop fix for Nat?

- Have you ever seen someone use oil to fix something?

Fluency

- Pick a page that most of the group read quite easily. Ask them to reread it with pace and expression. Model how to do this if necessary.

- Ask children to read pages 15–16 with lots of expression, paying attention to the ellipsis (e.g. building up expectation with a pause) and the exclamation mark.

- Practise reading the words on page 17.

Tricky words review

of	and	are
the	out	all
to	he	go
we	old	so
your	too	his